W9-BEC-794

Yellow Umbrella Books are published by Red Brick Learning
7825 Telegraph Road, Bloomington, Minnesota 55438
http://www.redbricklearning.com

Library of Congress Cataloging-in-Publication Data
Ring, Susan.
    [On all kinds of days. Spanish & English]
    On all kinds of days/by Susan Ring = Nos divertimos/por Susan Ring.
    p. cm.
    Summary: "Simple text and photos present the seasonal weather cycle and
activities to do in each season"—Provided by publisher.
    Includes bibliographical references and index.
    ISBN-13: 978-0-7368-6012-3 (hardcover)
    ISBN-10: 0-7368-6012-6 (hardcover)
    1. Weather—Juvenile literature. I. Title: Nos divertimos. II. Title.
QC981.3.R5618 2006
551.6—dc22   2005025842

Written by Susan Ring
Developed by Raindrop Publishing

Editorial Director: Mary Lindeen
Editor: Jennifer VanVoorst
Photo Researcher: Wanda Winch
Adapted Translations: Gloria Ramos
Spanish Language Consultants: Jesús Cervantes, Anita Constantino
Conversion Assistants: Jenny Marks, Laura Manthe

Photo Credits
Cover: Bernd Mohr; Title Page: Gary Sundermeyer/Capstone Press; Page 4: Gary
Sundermeyer/Capstone Press; Page 6: EyeWire; Page 8: Comstock; Page 10: Ron
Chapple/Thinkstock; Page 12: Nancy White/Capstone Press; Page 14: Comstock;
Page 16: Gary Sundermeyer/Capstone Press

1 2 3 4 5 6 11 10 09 08 07 06

On All Kinds of Days

by Susan Ring

Nos divertimos

por Susan Ring

Yellow Umbrella Books

for early readers

On sunny days
we ride our bikes.

En días de sol
andamos en bicicletas.

On rainy days
we splash in puddles.

En días de lluvia
salpicamos en los charcos.

On snowy days
we build a snowman.

En días de nieve hacemos
un muñeco de nieve.

On windy days
we fly kites.

En días de viento
volamos papalotes.

On hot days
we go for a swim.

En días
de calor nadamos.

On cold days
we stay inside.

En días de frío
nos quedamos adentro.

On all kinds of days
we can have fun.

Nos divertimos todos
los días.

Index

Índice

18